WHAT MAKES GREAT ATHLETES?

BY C.A. BARNHART

PEARSON

Scott
Foresman

Editorial Offices: Glenview, Illinois • Parsippany, New Jersey • New York, New York
Sales Offices: Needham, Massachusetts • Duluth, Georgia • Glenview, Illinois
Coppell, Texas • Ontario, California • Mesa, Arizona

ISBN: 0-328-13561-5

Althea Gibson in motion at Wimbledon, 1956

What is it about an athlete's performance that impresses other people so much? How is it that only a few people are able to become really fine athletes? What is it about athletic performances that make us admire athletes so much?

Consider television. Today we can watch a game unfold as it's happening, with all its surprises. We can soar with an outfielder as he jumps for a high fly ball that seems out of reach. We can smile with admiration at the height, grace, and form of a ballplayer's jump as he makes a catch. Watching feels like the closest thing to scooping up the ball ourselves. Experiences such as these allow us to witness the skill, ability, drive, and determination it takes to make the greatest athletes reach their highest goals.

Lisa Leslie, 2000 Olympics (USA vs. Australia)

Look at the **coordination** of this basketball team. Passing the ball is no simple act. You must keep the opposing team off-guard while keeping your eye on your own teammates. Now, pivot to the right, now to the left. Suddenly, from the stands, we see the ball arch overhead and sail right through the basket.

How do they do that? How do they make it look so simple and effortless?

It is an art to master a sport. We admire the teamwork, strategy, and coordination that produces a score. The combination of many factors creates moments of excitement. Fans shout and cheer at the accuracy of every shot.

Watch how a rider, high on a powerful horse, holds the reins loosely as if they were fine silk ribbons. We wince when a horse misses a jump or balks, and we ooh and ahh when a rider guides her horse to clear every jump.

Simona Amanar of Romania at the 2000 Olympics in
Sydney, Australia

Take the sport of gymnastics. At top speed, a
gymnast takes an exquisite tumble into a perfect
routine of jumps, leaps, cartwheels, or somersaults.

Television coverage has put sports in the limelight
and sparked an interest in sports that were not
popular in our culture, such as cricket, soccer, and
rugby. It would be a mistake, however, to believe
that television is solely responsible for the great
interest in sports. Before the days of television,
sporting events were reported in newspapers
and later on radio. Sports writers and announcers
described as many exciting happenings as possible.
People have always had a passion for sports, either
as participants, observers, or both.

Even in ancient times, athletes were greatly admired, and they occupied special positions in their societies. Consider the gladiators of Rome who entertained the Roman public in the **Colosseum**.

The gladiators were highly trained athletes who followed strict exercise routines and were given special food and drink. They were held in high **esteem** and honored with gifts by the Romans.

Much of our interest in sports and athletes comes from our knowledge of sporting events in ancient Greece. The first Olympics were held at least 2,800 years ago, and scholars believe that such games were probably held before then. The games were held at Olympia, a center of religious ceremonies, in honor of Zeus, the most powerful of the Greek gods. Only the Greeks competed in the original games.

Those early games were festivals that combined races with religious observances. Contests were added over time to include boxing, wrestling, and a pentathlon that included the discus and javelin throw.

The history of the Olympics started with the athletic ability of the gladiators, like this Samnite gladiator in full dress.

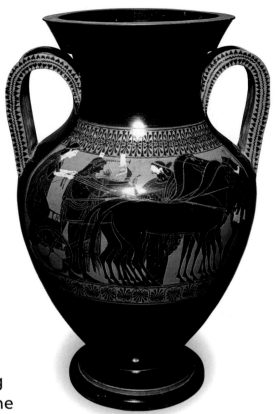

An ancient amphora was often the Olympic winner's prize.

Originally, only young men could compete in the Olympics. There is evidence, however, that at some point women competed in chariot races. An Olympic winner was honored much as today's athletes are recognized. Sometimes, a statue was made of the winner and placed near the Temple of Zeus. Athletes would also receive large sums of money from the cities they came from, and some were given a free meal each day for the rest of their lives.

In Greece, most athletes were in the military. They were kept physically fit by their service. From **artifacts**, such as decorated jars and cups that have been found by **archaeologists**, it is clear that the Greeks admired physical strength and ability in their athletes.

In about A.D. 100, the Greek philosopher Epictetus wrote about the training an athlete had to endure. He said that an athlete must obey his trainer. The athlete would eat only certain foods, work out regardless of the weather, and be willing to endure injuries and the shame of losing. Epictetus also said that a true athlete must give all his energy, skill, and passion to the contest. Though written two thousand years ago, Epictetus's words sound familiar to anyone who knows the effort and dedication it takes to become a fine athlete.

It's an old idea to see sports as a way of measuring a person's character. It's also an old, cherished idea that sports develop and strengthen the human individual and his or her sense of identity. Athletes are a privileged part of a long history of thrilling sports achievement. Today's athletes continue to bring honor and prestige to their homelands while inspiring people and nations the world over.

The boxer, attributed to Appolonius

Competition is about measuring yourself against others and constantly trying to improve. All sports require great effort and concentration. This is true whether it is Texan Lance Armstrong, today's seven-time bicycling champion and legend of the Tour de France, or Pheidippides of ancient Greece.

Pheidippides was a professional runner whose job was to carry messages for the Greek army. During the battle of Marathon, when the Greek forces were under attack by the Persians, Pheidippides had to run to Athens and warn Athenians that a Persian army was headed their way. Pheidippides was chosen because, as a professional runner, he would get there quickly. He successfully delivered the message but then died on the spot from exhaustion.

The modern marathon race, the last event of the Olympics, honors Pheidippides and his heroic achievement. Today's marathon race is just over twenty-six miles, but Pheidippides ran farther. He first ran 149 miles to Sparta to tell the Spartans that the Persians were attacking Greece. Then, after two more runs, he made his final, fatal run to Athens.

The marathon is the ultimate test for a long distance runner. In the 2004 Olympics held in Athens, Greece, Stefano Baldini, from Italy, won after a spectator at the race pushed another runner to the sidelines. The race took place during hot weather, and many runners dropped out from exhaustion. This is not unusual. The course is over hills and difficult terrain.

We do not know if Pheidippides was someone who liked running from the time he was young. We do know that he became a messenger known for his speed and **endurance** as an adult. Every athlete, whether professional or amateur, must have a special skill at some athletic ability, and have the desire to work to constantly improve his or her performance.

Italy's Stefano Baldini wins the men's marathon at the 2004 Olympics.

Jim Thorpe
in the 1912
Olympics,
Stockholm,
Sweden

The work of an athlete means putting aside other activities and devoting a large amount of time to practice. Yet many athletes feel happiest when they are engaged in their sport.

In the early twentieth century, there was a great "all-round" athlete named Jim Thorpe. He was born in Oklahoma. An energetic child, he'd often run the twenty miles home from school. He once said, "I never was content unless I was trying my skill in some game against my fellow playmates or testing my endurance and wits against some member of the animal kingdom."

It is not hard to imagine that this natural athlete's training was probably all about chasing rabbits or racing schoolmates. When he was in school in Pennsylvania, however, he easily cleared a high jump bar set at five feet nine inches while wearing work clothes, not shorts or athletic shoes.

Babe Didrikson won the hurdles and javelin competitions in the 10th Olympic Games held in California in 1932.

Another natural athlete of the twentieth century was Babe Didrikson Zaharias from Texas. By the time she was in her teens, she already knew she wanted to be the greatest athlete ever. She had this dream at a time when it was considered unusual for women to be athletes.

Babe thrived on competition and focused on winning. She also liked being in the limelight as a fine female competitor. She was extremely well coordinated and very strong mentally and physically. She could master track events without special training, and she easily won the javelin and the 80-meter hurdles events at the Olympics. She nearly won the high-jump event. After her career as a track and field champion, she became a professional golfer.

Not all Olympic champions ride smoothly to their goal, however. After Thorpe won his gold medals at the Olympics, the committee took back his medals because of a technicality—he had been paid to play football for a local team. Thorpe never recovered from that disappointment, even though he had a second career as a professional football player. Babe Didrikson Zaharias also had to deal with disappointment. In the Olympic high-jump event, the judges threw out one of her jumps on a technicality, and she had to settle for a silver medal instead of a gold.

Most great athletes, however, reach success as a result of natural ability, tremendous **persistence**, and **rigorous** training. Usually when young children begin to take up sports, abilities start showing up. Gym teachers and coaches notice a young person who has a natural ability to run, swim, shoot baskets, or balance on the balance beam. Parents also notice when their child likes a particular sport and has a knack for doing it well. If the child begins to work seriously at swimming, for example, often what happens is that the better he or she gets, the more the young person wants to work on it. In addition, many athletes tell of being inspired to want to train and compete.

Training is intended to strengthen muscles, focus concentration, and increase control. Training exercises are part of a daily routine, which may often seem boring. The athlete in training must learn to listen to advice from coaches and be willing to try new ways of doing things. In the end, however, the athlete must decide whether such training is rewarding enough to keep at it. If the athlete feels too stressed or overburdened by serious training, winning an event or gaining recognition and praise will not be great enough rewards.

When we watch another person do something well, it looks easy. What shows is an athlete's **mastery**, and that is the result of a great deal of practice and training. All of the work—the throbbing, aching muscles that come from workouts—is not what we see. In the case of the athlete, we see and admire the athlete's mastery of his or her body in accomplishing the sport.

A weightlifter demonstrates weightlifting techniques.

No athlete achieves success just by wishing for it. Ice skaters often have to get up early in the morning to practice at a rink before the school day begins. They must be ready to go through exercise routines that are the same day after day. They must be willing to try something new without hesitation, to listen to criticism, and to pay close attention to the smallest detail of performance in order to get it right.

Another difficult part of being an athletic competitor is knowing that even though you have done your very best, you may not win. Learning to face the disappointment of loss and still continue competing at top form and with total concentration is not easy.

David Pelletier and Jamie Sale perform in the 2002 Winter Olympics.

The athlete's life is not easy. Competing in the Olympics or on the school field, working hard to become a good competitor, and having to face losing are all difficult challenges. These difficulties often become reasons for talented young athletes to decide that competition is not for them. It takes strength of character and determination to keep competing at higher and higher levels.

At the competitions prior to the Olympics, the best entrants in each event improve their chances to enter the Olympics. Imagine what it is like to intensively prepare to be an Olympic competitor, winning nearly every event you have entered and then facing athletes from all over the world. Facing other highly trained athletes and winning is the greatest thrill and makes it all worthwhile.

Throughout history, civilizations have recognized the importance of exercise and fitness. Physical training has been a part of general education programs for thousands of years. As early as 2500 B.C., the Chinese were making physical exercise a part of education. This was even earlier than the Greeks, who inspired the development of European and American sports.

Most of us do not compete in the Olympic Games; many of us never compete in athletic events at all. Yet active nonathletes can benefit from being involved in athletics. Athletics improve mental and physical capacities whether one wants to become an athlete or not. It is healthy to develop daily exercise routines and weekly fitness regimens. Exercise and sports activities contribute greatly to one's overall well-being. We can all admire the superior athletic qualities in the greatest athletes.

U.S. artistic gymnasts in Athens, Greece, 2004.

Now Try This

You have read about what makes a great athlete. It's clear that athletic success does not happen overnight. It takes forming a plan and practicing long hours. There are also many kinds of athletes and many approaches to sports.

Choose a sport in which you'd like to participate. Can you think of a training program that would help you improve your performance? Or, if you're not sure about which sport is right for you, make some plans for teaching yourself more about sports.

Tryouts for competitions can be a crowded situation.

Here's How to Do It!

1. Write out a plan for training that is challenging but not impossible to follow.

2. Mark off a distance to run. Have a friend time you as you run the distance. Try to figure out what helps you perform better.

3. Become a sports reporter for your class. Write about athletic events at your school or in your community. You could interview different athletes. Find out what they like about athletics.

4. Imagine you are a competitor in a particular event that interests you at the Olympic Games. Write an imaginary journal about what it is like to compete, how you feel as you start your race or performance and, if you won, what that was like. Do the same as if you lost, and record how you felt about it.

Glossary

archaeologists *n.* those who study ancient people and their civilizations.

artifacts *n.* things made by people for a special use, such as pottery or tools.

Colosseum *n.* a large building with high banks of seats that could hold many people to watch an event in ancient Rome.

coordination *n.* a working together.

endurance *n.* the strength to last and withstand hard wear or work.

esteem *v.* to regard with favorable opinion or admiration.

mastery *n.* great skill or knowledge.

persistence *n.* the act of not giving up on something, of continuing.

rigorous *adj.* strict and demanding.